The Yes Symphonies

J O

BookLeaf
Publishing

India | USA | UK

Presentation by *BookLeaf Publishing*

Web: www.bookleafpub.com

E-mail: info@bookleafpub.com

ISBN: 9789357447003

First edition 2022

DEDICATION

To J. Who has tapped into my universe.

Belief

Belief
Belief in you
Belief in me
Belief in we
Belief inside
Growth of a tribe

Soft Meat

Running of the fingers through plumage
A soft green leaf
Perched atop a force to be reckoned with
Pluck it off
The transformation begins
Two hands
Gripping and digging
Feasting and yearning
Where does the goddess go?
Where does the light exist?
Far beyond the fruit trees
Into the sky
An eruption so sweet
It goes beyond the mind's eye

Event Horizon

Kneel and never rise
Understand the heightened quality
Of what lies between these thighs
I could move mountains
I could quiet oceans
I could make wind still
I could lift heavens
I could pause time
But I can't make you stop
When you're at that line

The Grotto

Where would you look for me?
Would you look in the dense tree bark?
Would you separate the wheat rows?
Would you find me in the earthy soil
Smelling of life and now.
Would you seek me out in vineyards nestled
With berries that exist to be squeezed.
Can you hear my yes symphonies in the
darkened hours?
Can you feel the ruptures and eruptions?
Seismic waves with no measurements, no highs
and no lows.
Steady vibrations seeping love everywhere
With no culmination. No stoppage time no
fruition.

Pressure

Coax it out of me
The muffled sigh
The tight holds
The yearning cries
Tame what is untamable
The begging falls on cosmos' door
The twist of torsos
Of Athena's arrows
Plunging into chests
Coax it out of me
What diamonds are made from

So Below

Where is the woman hopping the fence into
oblivion?
Does she see what rocky path lies ahead.
No shoes, no clothes, no eyes left to look
She climbs mountains bare bodied and restless.
She crosses valleys thighs wide with abandoned
compunction.
Her back is laced with strings of impunity from
a freedom she declines.
She seeks him out, wild haired and wide eyed.
Sweat and sighs and agitation build.
Finally a tree is found, fallen and wide.
She lies down and takes her place.

Impatience

A sinless confession cries out
The flowers open
The ground hums
No sound is made
But the rhythm of earth's drums.
A falling here, a rise there.
Waves are crashing and the lights dim.
Fluttering shut and fluttering closed.
No release no direction. Where is my savior with
my resurrection?

Thick Air

Golden hued days bring
Flame lit nights.
A wash of heat never leaves the air and the night
still tastes like the sun.
An endless supply for an endless thirst.
The drink slides down slow, familiar and
needed.
The heat rises, the seats stay occupied.
A crescendo of warmth, it's now unbearable but
it remains unbroken.
Eyes fixed on the prize a long sweet swig and
the thirst remains unquenched. Stay seated or sit
somewhere else.

Rev. 6:1-2

A happy death
But a torturous exit.
An opening of God's grace
But an ecstasy of panic.
Internal combustion and contortion happily
marry, creating a universe unknown to any.
Put on a saddle, chomp on the bit, and ride the
horseman into your apocalypse.

Nirvana

Bless me Goddess for I have sinned.
I have laid myself bare.
I have opened my spring.
I have waded in waters this mortal brings.
I drink freely from a cup with no end.
I arch and bend north to the stars' five points
and I succumb to the direction of Mars.
I have gone beyond the tolls and I paid in brazen
currency.
I drew everything back for a ceaseless pouring
of wisdom.

Descent

This wall is strong
Heaves and pushing
Hoisting and pulling.
The cracks don't exist yet but give it time.
We're learning our thresholds don't exist.

The Yes Symphonies

What would the soundtrack be?
It would be soft breaths
And hard inhales.
Gasps and letters.
Four word sentences.
Four words.
Guttural escapes and high heaven trumpets.
Rapid and slow air.
True symphonies hushed in the background.
They don't compare.

Evolution

Amnesia sets in from a biological knock.
Where am I and who am I.
Cares are hauled away and all that's left is
what's right. All that remains is the primal.
It's mounting. It's increasing. Nothing is wrong.
Everything must be done. Everything must be
taken. Ask questions later. It's rocketing past the
dark galaxy. It's careening into white space.
Accept it and stay bare. Feel the seismology
shatter the macrocosm. The barriers are down.
How far are we? Just keep going.

Shroud

A fixture on the bed.
It tells a multitude of stories.
Each print, each wrinkle, each furrow.
A ruffle, a mark, an indentation.
A complex book with no words.
A movie with no pictures.
But a lifetime of conversation
Written on its canvas.
An indelible ink grown invisible with time.
But if words could be uttered
What obscenities would be said.
What curses would be spoken.
What promises would be made.
What cries would be stolen.
Love hexes
Sex spells
Ecstasy in mori.
Rebirth in time.

Prison

Scream at me
Gnaw at me
Dig at my flesh
And nestle yourself in my independence.
Shackle me freely and fight against your
resistance. Overcome me overwhelm me and
rebel from your righteousness.
Sprint towards divine cruelty
And bask in its justice. A sob so sweet escapes
from us both creating a new life. A new sound
echoes and emerges from a valley of thorns. A
prick and the spirit flows.
A letting of souls and a march into madness.

Traveler's Rest

Walk into the hinterland like a withered soldier
desperate of warm respite.
A stunning sight manifests
An oasis a haven.
Undo your binds and envelop yourself in the
hearth.
Wearily you emerge from blockades and
hungrily you enter into a timeless siege. You
thrust into the hilt with outcries of a fervor lost
in time. The horizons open
the stars fall from the sky. A chasm forms.
Wider wider. The boundary is pushed the
boundary is broken. When you walk into the
hinterland you never return.

Willing Subservience

Below the shallows
I return. Rebirth has begun.
A life of servitude
A glimpse of a chaotic heaven.
Bliss found from darkness
Light found from despair.
I was captured and then captivated
From a foreign place that took hold of me and
glared.
It bore into my cells, into the very fine spindle of
DNA.
A boulder of fantasies made.
Rolling in and rolling out
A frenetic cycle from which an end springs
further ends. Chased after and never satisfied.

Revolutionaries

One glance and I know you.
One flesh
One body
One sword of all.
Scars and bloodlines
Lines and creases.
A fading of duality
Immortality.
You'll find me next time
We're made the same now.
When I'm there you're there
When I'm here you're here.
My breath winds with yours
My folds close with yours.
Planets align Venus and Mars
Neptune and Pluto.
The underworld shakes and
Persephone breaks.
Hearts crushed beauty divine.
She stayed and he needed
He loved and she was dismayed.
It's only the beginning
Another journey to unfold.
We'll be catapulted into this time and that time.
You'll find me next time.

I'll find you next time.
You'll find me next time.